My Hollywood Adventure

by
Bonny the Shih Tzu

As barked to Jonathan Agronsky

Published in the United States by Buddha Dog Books. No part of this book may be reproduced in any form or by any means without permission from the publisher, except by a reviewer, who may quote brief passages in a review.

Library of Congress Cataloging-in-Publication Data

Agronsky, Jonathan

My Hollywood Adventure by Bonny the Shih Tzu/As Barked to Jonathan Agronsky

Cover Photo by Claire Doré
Book Design and Publishing Logo by James Lyon
Photography and Editorial Assistance by Claire Doré

Buddha Dog Books
P.O. Box 1476
Pinehurst, North Carolina 28370
Website: shihtzunation.com
e-mail: boodadog18@aol.com

ISBN-13: 978-0-692-02525-3
ISBN-10: 0-692-02525-1

ACKNOWLEDGEMENTS

I want to thank Aunt Cathy Pittman for adopting me, and for having enough faith in my potential acting abilities to put me up for a movie role within days of my rehoming. (What a big risk she took!) I was honored to then be made a member of her and Uncle Gregg's troupe of well-trained and well-loved animal actors. I hope I did you proud by my performance in Martin McDonagh's zany black comedy, "Seven Psychopaths," which is recounted in this book.

Speaking of Martin, I owe the Irish writer-director a debt of gratitude as well—not only for selecting me over half a dozen other Shih Tzu that were larger and arguably more glamorous than this teacup-sized Lion Dog raised in an East L.A. trailer park, but also for keeping me on the job after a classic display of Shih Tzu defiance on my one and only rehearsal day.

I also wish to thank the entire cast and crew of "Seven Psychopaths," who were incredibly patient and solicitous toward this four-legged performer throughout the filming. I am particularly grateful to Peter, the film's first assistant director, who at one point offered to adopt me; hairstylist Pauletta, who gave me a collar medallion that I shall treasure and wear always; human co-stars Colin Farrell, who came to my rescue when I strayed too close to a burning car on the movie set, and Christopher

Walken, who protected me from an overzealous fan at the movie's international premiere in Toronto.

A bark of gratitude goes out as well to Barbara Gordon, who opened up a whole new world to me when she enrolled me in the pet therapy program she founded, called R.O.M.P., which stands for Reconnecting With Our Military Personnel. After getting certified as a pet therapy dog, I've gone with her to veterans' health facilities in Los Angeles to share my puppy love with some of America's aging military heroes. I can't wait to go back again!

Thanks also to my co-author, Jonathan Agronsky, who used his deep understanding of and appreciation for the Shih Tzu breed, to give me an authentic canine voice.

I also wish to thank Miss Lola. Though she occasionally tries a little too hard to compete with me for my mom's attention, this sweet and funny Chihuahua-terrier mix is the only member of Claire's canine family whom I have unconditionally accepted into my pack. (I am very picky!) Today, I am happy to call her my BFLF (Best Four-Legged Friend).

Finally, I want to thank my mom, Miss Claire Doré, who has lovingly and patiently overseen my transformation from a little lost soul into a confident, well-trained, well-behaved, canine model and actress. From the moment I first encountered Claire, to this very day, she has made me feel loved, safe and welcome. You don't just rock my world, Mom, you are my world!

CONTENTS

Chapter 1
The Short Goodbye

Cute 1 year old shitzu *(sic)*. Very playful
and good with kids! She is a female and
up to date with her shots.
- Craigslist.org listing from
September 24, 2011

THE first thing the friendly, kind-hearted lady
who answered my mom's Craigslist ad did after
paying for me was to clean my little paws. Miss
Cathy Pittman noticed that I had stepped in a
pool of slimy green liquid outside my mom's

single-wide in East L.A. Fearing it might be antifreeze, which is a deadly poison, she had asked my mom for a bowl of warm, soapy water and a towel, then gone to work on me like Jesus washing the feet of his disciples. As Miss Cathy would later tell a friend, "I didn't want to pull up to the house and open up the kennel only to find that my new Shih Tzu puppy had gotten sick or even died on the way home."

"Home", I would learn, was the ranch owned by Miss Cathy and her man mate, Gregg, in California's Antelope Valley, about an hour north of L.A. Besides putting a roof over their heads, it served as headquarters for their company, Performing Animal Troupe, through which, by the time of my adoption, the now middle-aged couple had been supplying "well-trained and well-loved animal actors" for movies, television, videos, photography, and even live shows for nearly thirty years.

As it turned out, Miss Cathy needn't have worried about my state of physical health—my mom had taken very good care of me—but I'll admit I was kind of nervous after being picked up by a stranger, placed into a portable doggie dungeon and driven away to God knows where. I also felt sad and confused. Why had my mom suddenly decided to get rid of me?

Admittedly, I wasn't a perfect puppy. For one thing, at nine months old I still wasn't completely housebroken, but she should have known that we Shih Tzu are stubborn and notoriously hard to train. Other than those occasional mishaps, though, I can't think of anything else I might have done to make my mom mad at me. But humans, I've learned, sometimes do things that no self-respecting dog would ever do, like abandoning a loved one because caring for him or her no longer seemed practical or convenient.

Miss Cathy Pittman with one of her hundreds of "animal actors."

And, if you're a dog, when things turn out badly, other than running away, there's not a whole lot you can do about it. At that moment, escaping was out of the question. We Shih Tzu are very smart, but we're no Houdinis. I wondered how many other canine souls had preceded me in this crate, so full of doggie smells, and what had happened to each of them. As Miss Cathy's van wound its way out of the trailer park, I hunkered down in the back, quietly awaiting my fate.

Chapter 2
Are You My Mommy?

Bonding with my new Mom after a bath.

WHEN Miss Cathy eased her vehicle into the ranch's driveway, another woman was waiting. As soon as the van stopped, the second woman, younger, with long, dark hair, slid open the side door and liberated me from my travel crate. For the next few minutes, I walked around inside the van, more or less ignoring the shy, demure young woman who was about to become this puppy's new mom. Finally, Miss Claire Doré picked me up and held me, stroking and talking to me in a gentle, soothing voice. I just kind of lay there in her arms, didn't wag my tail or kiss her or otherwise show any excitement or emotion.

Claire then carried me inside the ranch house and into Miss Cathy and Mr. Gregg's office, where Miss Cathy briefed her about that evening's assignment. Then Claire put me down on the office floor and left. While she was gone, Miss Cathy cuddled me and offered me some kibble, but I was too nervous to eat.

Eventually, Claire reappeared and loaded me back into the kennel, which she carried outside and placed into the company van, alongside two other crates containing a pair of Performing Animal Troupe cats. Claire had trained the feline actors, who were going to appear in an episode of "Dexter," a TV series about a serial killer who works for the police as a blood spatter analyst. By bringing me along on the shoot, which was to be staged at a home in Burbank, California, that very evening, my new mom had thus immediately begun the long, arduous process of "socializing" me—something my original mom had done

6

precious little of during the more than six months she had kept me, confined much of the time to the trailer's tiny laundry area.

When we arrived in Burbank, Claire busied herself with the cats. At least for the moment, I got to chill in my crate, which was fine with me. The plastic animal carrier had quickly become my safe zone, a place where I could gather my thoughts and do whatever I wanted to—which was to sleep, mostly—so long as it didn't involve traveling! This peaceful hiatus, however, didn't last long. Whenever there was a break in the filming, my new mom freed me from my kennel, placed me on a lead and walked me around the movie set, where I saw scary-looking creatures with big glass eyes (I later would learn they're called "klieg lights") and other exotic things that humans apparently use to create these elaborate daydreams they call movies.

Despite the novelty of my surroundings, the strange sights and smells and people moving around me, I pretended to take everything and everyone new in stride, as if this were all routine stuff for me—which it most certainly was not. But why should I let anyone else know that? I am, after all, a Shih Tzu. As a breed, we pride ourselves on maintaining our dignity and decorum at all times. Nothing less would be acceptable from a descendant of the mythical Lion Dog that once provided companionship and protection to Lord Buddha. After the filming was completed, Claire packed up the cats and me and drove us all to her ranch house, a few miles down the road from the Pittmans' ranch. There she introduced me, two at a time, to her six other dogs. First, she brought in "Lola," a scruffy Chihuahua-terrier mix who was the only dog smaller than I was, and "Cognac," an apricot-colored miniature poodle. I more or less ignored them until they both tried to sniff my butt, whereupon I calmly walked away. Happily, they didn't seem put off by this newcomer's diffidence, and just kind of ignored me in return. Next up came "Skippy," a Jack Russell mix, and a Papillon named "Maestro." They too tried to do the sniffy-sniffy and, once again, I let it be known that this girl's bottom was off limits, thank you very much, so kindly leave me the heck alone. They, too, seemed content to give me my space, as did Claire's remaining two dogs, a red-coated Golden Retriever named "Owen," and a medium-sized terrier mix named "Iris." It's amazing how tolerant other dogs can be when you're clever enough *not* to present yourself to them in a dominant fashion. I was way too smart—and small, and cautious—to unnecessarily provoke them.

As for Claire's nine resident cats, I simply ignored them all.

When it was time for bed, Claire did something very sweet—and surprising, considering that the newest member of her resident dog pack, moi, had arrived in its midst just hours earlier: She took me to bed with her. Or should I say with her and three of her other doggies, all of whom she treats like four-legged kids. Though I didn't let on, being included in this intimate family group did not comfort me, as I'm sure my new mom intended it to; in fact, it made me kind of nervous. You see, I had had almost no experience interacting with other dogs, and I didn't know if they would wait until I fell asleep and tear my throat out, or what. I slept with one eye open, and when everyone, including Claire, was snoozing away, I crept off the bed onto the floor, and spent the remainder of the night there. That way, nobody would get jealous and, if anyone decided to get cute with me any way during the night, I would be able to see them coming and thus be ready to defend myself.

Chapter 3
Not Too L.A.

*One look and Martin McDonagh knew I was the one
he was looking for.*

THE next morning, more big surprises were in
store for this four-legged shut-in, who had rarely
had the run of my mom's trailer, let alone the

expanses of Greater Los Angeles, including the
world-renowned movie lots and shooting locations
where Claire and other "studio animal trainers"
routinely worked their magic before the cameras.
Before leaving the house, Claire packed me, a
Japanese Chin named "Delilah," another Shih
Tzu mix, and a miniature poodle into separate
kennels, then drove us to the offices of CBS Films
in Burbank, California, where we were scheduled
for an 11 a.m. "showing." As Claire carried our
kennels into the empty room and lined them up
against the back wall, the five film company
bigwigs who had assembled there eyeballed the
containers as if they expected Peggy Lee to pop
out of one of them and start purring: "Is that all
there is? Is that all there is? Cause if that's all
there is, my friend, let's keep on dancing."

Instead, Claire took us out of our carriers one
by one, leashed us up and paraded us before the
folks who apparently would have to decide if any
of us seemed right for the part of "Bonny" the
Shih Tzu in an upcoming movie called "Seven
Psychopaths." The group included the film's first
assistant director, who would develop a huge
crush on me during shooting—but I'm getting
ahead of myself. The movie people also picked
each of us up and held us in their arms to see

11

how we'd react to being handled by a stranger. Apparently, I made quite an impression on the film's writer-director, Martin McDonagh, who comes from a faraway land that I understand has no snakes but plenty of leprechauns. A tall, lean, intense-looking man with close-cropped hair and a mischievous glint in his beady blue eyes that betrayed his deeply satirical take on the world, Martin announced at the end of the hour-long session: "Well, it looks like we have our Bonny."

Martin McDonagh has impeccable taste in dogs.

According to Martin, who previously had rejected five larger and more glamorous Shih Tzu Claire had brought to him because he'd found them "all too frou-frou, all too L.A," this trailer park Shih Tzu, eight pounds dripping wet, was "just perfect" for the role. "She has these funny little eyes," he said, unflatteringly, "with one going in one direction, and one going off in another. She was a scraggly little—what do you call them? Saved? Rescue. As soon as I saw her, I knew she was the one."

Claire of course was thrilled that Martin had chosen me. But she also was anxious. She knew that filming of Martin's zany black comedy was scheduled to begin in just five short weeks, and she somehow would have to transform this newly rehomed, barely socialized Shih Tzu puppy, who also happened to be a total newcomer to the world of showbiz, into a disciplined, obedient, above all, reliable performer.

I would not have traded places with her for a ton of bacon bits.

Chapter 4

Color Me Clueless

Initially a rival, Lola, the Chihuahua mix, would become my Best Four-Legged Friend, or BFLF.

IN less than 24 hours, this "scraggly" Shih Tzu with the "funny little eyes" had not only been snatched out of her small but familiar world and exposed to a host of new people, places and experiences, I also had been chosen to star in what folks out here on the Coast call a "major motion picture," Hollywood jargon for a film in which someone is willing to invest millions of dollars. On the other hand, I soon would learn, there was a lot of work to be done before this canine Cinderella would be ready to attend the royal ball and dance with the likes of Christopher Walken, Colin Farrell, and Woody Harrelson, to name just a few of my human co-stars in "Seven Psychopaths." First and foremost, my new mom had to form a bond of trust with a dog who not only had had little experience interacting with people, but who also, in her words, was "despondent," "didn't make eye contact" with anyone, "didn't know how to play, didn't know how to interact with other dogs," and "just wanted to kind of lay around."

So much for positive first impressions!

One thing soon became clear: There'd be very little "laying around" anymore for this sheltered Shih Tzu. In order to "socialize" me, Claire took me everywhere with her, both on and off the job. She encouraged me to interact with everyone we met, whether that individual happened to get around on two legs or four. Regarding the two-legged ones, there was a certain irony in this situation, given the fact that Claire, like me, is by nature calm, quiet and self-contained. So, I guess we both were getting something out of these frequent contacts, especially when the people we met were strangers to her as well as to me. In fact, it would not be too big a stretch to suggest that this shared personality trait helped strengthen the bond that was beginning to be forged between the two of us. Here we were, two kindred souls bravely facing the world together.

Although I was mostly cooperating with Claire's efforts to socialize me, there was one area in which I would not play along. Starting on the day I was adopted, I absolutely, one hundred percent refused to eat. No amount of sweet-talking could get me to ingest even a single bite of kibble, let alone any of the dog treats my new mom had offered me. When I kept up my hunger strike for the next two days, Claire and Miss Cathy feared I might be sick (remember the green slime I had stepped in at the trailer park?). They were so concerned, in fact, that they took me to a veterinarian to get me checked out. The vet, of course, gave me a clean bill of health. His diagnosis? "She's a Shih Tzu," he explained. "They can be very stubborn."

While the animal doctor might have accurately described my behavior, he could not say what was driving it. The fact is, despite the many kindnesses that Claire and Miss Cathy, Claire's other dogs—and most everyone else I had encountered after leaving the trailer park—had shown to me, I did not yet believe in my heart of hearts that the new world into which I suddenly had been thrust was an entirely safe and trustworthy place. Once that situation changed, I figured, there'd be plenty of time to fill my tummy.

Meanwhile, I'd put my new mom on notice that training the newest member of Performing Animal Troupe was going to be anything but routine.

Chapter 5
Critters of the Mass Bark

*Miss Cathy with PeeWee the dancing horse
and trainers Miss Janis and Miss Carol.*

NOT to brag or anything, but I think I did a
pretty amazing job keeping my cool during my

first extended visit to Mr. Gregg and Miss Cathy Pittman's ranch in Palmdale, California, a two-and-a-half acre spread where the middle-aged couple lives with their son, Justin, and more than one hundred members of their Performing Animal Troupe, each of whom they consider to be a member of their extended animal family. As in any family, I'd learn, certain members inevitably get special treatment. In the Pittmans' case, that was reserved for the ten dogs and a cat that back then had the run of the ranch house, including more than half a dozen Chihuahuas, the closest thing to a rat, if you ask me, in the canine world. The rat pack gave me a deafening welcome that was so disconcerting even to Claire that she picked me up and carried me into the Pittmans' quaintly decorated home office, then closed the door to keep them at bay. After calm was restored, I got to look around the room, whose walls were filled with photographs and other colorful mementos of the more than thirty years Mr. Gregg and Miss Cathy had spent working together on the animal side of showbiz.

For instance, I saw a picture of Miss Cathy standing next to Henry Winkler (a.k.a. "the Fonz") and an elephant on the back lot of the TV series, "Sabrina the Teenage Witch." There was a giant cardboard cut-out of "Mindy," a German shepherd/collie mix from the company who appeared in the movie "Bowfinger," wearing high-heeled shoes. Next to it was a photo of the multi-talented Steve Martin, who had signed it for Mr.

Gregg. Other photos showed actor Alec Baldwin with the troupe's oldest dog, a pug named "Pugsley," who had appeared with the star of "30 Rock" in a 1999 movie called "Thick as Thieves." My favorite picture of all, though, was of a very handsome beagle named "Breezy," who appeared in the "Star Trek: Enterprise" television series, as the Captain's dog, "Porthos."

This is one of the many souvenirs of their acting gigs displayed in Miss Cathy and Mr. Gregg's ranch house office.

Despite her initial caution, Claire soon re-opened the office door and we quickly were joined in the room by rat pack members "Chester," "Mike," "Bob," "Tootsie," "Billy," "Ricky," "Rocko" and "Vinny" (the latter two, I'm almost certain, belonged to the canine mafia), along with a Pomeranian named "Quigley" and a mixed terrier named "Paxton." As far as I was concerned, Claire's total immersion canine socialization strategy was growing old fast; but, even with the onslaught of strange new critters literally on my tail, I managed to put on an outward show of calmness and dignity that denied the rat pack any opportunity to intimidate me, if that indeed was their goal.

Claire would later ascribe my actions to the fact that, regardless of what is happening around me, I always manage to stay in my "own little world;" but I would prefer to believe that my actions reflect the fact that I always do whatever I have to do in order to master my environment. If that requires me to ignore everyone or everything vying for my attention at any particular point in time, then so be it. I have always preferred having the world bend to accommodate me rather than the other way around. Such an attitude, by the way, is not uncommon in dogs of my particular bloodline; not that many centuries ago, the Shih Tzu was the pampered pet of Chinese emperors, resting in his Majesty's silken sleeves while he sat upon his throne weighing grave matters of state, and dining on quail breasts, antelope milk and other rare delicacies fed to her by the palace eunuchs.

Fortunately, Claire did not feel obliged—either during my initial visit to the ranch or, I'm happy to say, on any subsequent visits—to further test my confidence or composure by involuntarily acquainting me with any of the larger or weirder creatures who made their home there. I cannot imagine what I would do, for instance, were she to place me in proximity of the Pittmans' parrots, rabbits, goats, sheep, pigs, donkeys, horses or llamas. Noble breeding notwithstanding, there is only so much novelty a girl can be introduced to at any one given moment before totally losing it. I believe that my new mom could sense my limitations in this regard, and I can only hope that Claire does not change her mind one day and try to take her Shih Tzu socialization campaign one species too far. If she does, incidentally, I will be soooo out of here!

22

Chapter 6
Excuse Me: You Want Me To Do *What*?!

"She does whatever she feels like, in true Shih Tzu fashion. Obedience is not her strong suit. Independence is."

- Claire Doré on training Bonny

"You realize, of course, that my ancestors were worshipped by Buddhist monks?"

THERE are certain virtues in a routine, predictable, uneventful life. When I lived with my original mom, for instance, I always knew what to expect. There were no unpleasant surprises, no big demands made on me. I just kind of did my thing, hung out by myself during the day while she worked, then tried to amuse her as much as I could during the short time we spent together each evening before she went to bed. Every once in a while, her daughter and granddaughter would visit, and I'd get to play with the urchin, which provided just enough of a break from the same-old-same-old routine to make my lonely, isolated life bearable.

Nowadays, I have scant time to ruminate on that 'other life,' which, though only weeks away in time, sometimes seems so far away and long ago that it never really happened. From the time I wake up each day till the time I hit the sack along with my new fur brothers and sisters, I spend every waking moment with my new mom, who is constantly either introducing me to someone new or trying to train me. With regard to the latter pursuit, I have to admit that, had our roles been reversed and I had been placed in charge of transforming this somewhat spoiled, headstrong, "unsocialized" Shih Tzu into a responsible, obedient canine actor in just five short weeks, I almost certainly would have packed up my kibbles in a doggie saddlebag and hit the road. Poor Claire, of course, did not have that luxury.

Instead of bemoaning her fate, however, she simply rolled up her sleeves and got to work.

While maintaining the charming façade befitting my breed, I made it very clear to Claire that merely dipping into her standard bag of doggie training tricks was not going to get her the results she was seeking. I showed absolutely no interest in toys, for example, nor did I have much use for the praise and affection she heaped on me whenever I happened to do something—not intentionally, mind you—that she wanted me to. She was certainly not going to try bullying me into following her commands. This would have gone violently against both her style and her temperament—which left her with one final option: bribing me with food. (Of course, you'll never catch Claire or any other trainer who uses positive reinforcement to train their charges, using such a term; they prefer to say they are "rewarding" the animal for the desired behavior.)

Naturally, I made even that most reliable of all trainer fallbacks challenging for Claire. It took her a week and a half just to find out what sort of treats I was willing to "work for." What surprised her even more than how long it took her to crack the appetite code, however, was the kind of savory treat that I preferred. Rather than the beef, liver or chicken that got most dogs salivating like Pavlov's famous laboratory subjects, Claire discovered that I preferred plain kibble and beef jerky from Costco (I knew instantly if the latter was not my favorite brand and would quickly spit it out if it wasn't.) Even after learning what I liked to eat, however, Claire had to use yet another trick of the trade—offering the treat to another dog who was standing nearby and thus denying it to me—in order to get me to finally accept it from her.

Sometimes, to break up the training monotony, my mom lets me practice my commands—such as "paw" shown here—in unusual settings, such as perched on the head of this life-sized bear statue.

26

Amazingly—and I promise you, people, no one was more surprised than I was—Claire not only got me to accept the food rewards, she eventually was able to link them up to my responses to such basic commands as "sit," "on your feet" (stand up), "down" (lie down), "speak," "paw" (shake hands), and "stay." She even trained me to "go to a mark," a rather laborious process in which I eventually learned to run over to a small square and put my front paws on it. (Even human movie actors, I'd learn, have to do this successfully in order to get their food rewards, which they call "lunch.")

To teach me this particular stunt, Claire first got me to run up to a wooden box and perch on top of it with my two front paws. Then she gradually made the mark I was aiming for smaller and less substantial, until it was just a small square of tile or wood. I don't know if she was a genius for figuring out how to get me to do this, or I was a genius for learning how to do it; but I can tell you this: By the time those five weeks of intensive training and socialization had ended, there was nothing I would not do for Claire—and, it seemed, nothing she would not do for me. And it had a whole lot more to do with the fact that I had fallen paws over tail in love with this gentle, patient, lovely, two-legged creature than with anything she had been feeding me.

Um, did I mention that, while all of this was happening, Claire was still trying to housebreak me?

Chapter 7
Lights, Camera . . . Woof!

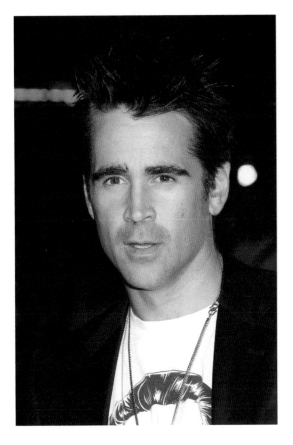

During rehearsals, I refused to kiss Hollywood heartthrob Colin Farrell, shown here at the L.A. "Seven Psychopaths" premiere in October 2012.

IN November 2011, just five weeks after fate had thrust me into a brave new world of people, animals, tricks and commands, I got my chance to show everyone who had put something on the line for me—whether time, money, effort, or affection—that she or he had invested wisely. Being a Lion Dog, however, I did not want to make things too easy on my human benefactors, lest they too hastily conclude that they, rather than this undersized Shih Tzu puppy, were in control.

Okay, I'll admit my new mom harbored no such illusions. In fact, I kept poor Claire guessing about what I would do when Martin McDonagh barked, "Action!" and the cameras began to roll. What made things even more "interesting" (in the Chinese sense of the word) for her was that my natural inclination to do things *my* way was just the icing on the cake of troubles she already had tasted. Normally, she would have three to six months in which to prepare a novice dog like me for an acting gig. But in my case, she had just over a month. Adding to her understandable anxiety was the unsettling fact that, on rehearsal day, I had declined to perform a simple trick she had taught me, one we had successfully rehearsed together dozens of times before.

In that opening scene, my job was to stand on the chest of Colin Farrell, who plays a down-on-his-luck Hollywood screenwriter named "Marty," who is sleeping off a drunk at his friend "Billy's" house after being kicked out of his girlfriend's apartment. I was to lick Marty's face until he wakes up. I did just fine in the rehearsal until it was time to kiss the Irish heartthrob. Although I'm sure Colin's legion of female fans will find this hard to believe, I declined to take a lick. I demurred despite the fact that Claire had just daubed Colin's face with beef-flavored baby food. The classic dog trainer's ruse had worked well when Claire tested it on Gregg and Justin Pittmans' faces at the ranch. But by the time rehearsals rolled around, I had grown tired of the flavor.

Needless to say, this did not go down well with the director, who had an assistant phone Claire as she was driving home to remind her that it was unacceptable for the dog they had hired *not* to follow the script exactly as it was written. Claire, of course, assured the caller that I would be ready to fulfill my contractual obligations when filming on "Seven Psychopaths" began—on the very next day. Then she went into what she calls "hurry-up mode" to try to resolve the crisis I had created.

First stop was the neighborhood grocery store, where Claire bought several jars of meat-flavored baby food, along with gravy-based dog and people food. Fortunately, her housemate had a sense of humor, because he good-naturedly allowed her to take a sponge and daub half a dozen of her samples on his face, one at a time, to see if I would lick any of them off. When my mom tried

Gerber's pork-flavored baby food, it was like, Bingo! By the time that discovery was made, both of us were more than ready to crash. It had been the longest working day in my short life and obviously had been an especially taxing one for Claire. As always, I slept like a rock; but when I woke up briefly in the middle of the night, I saw her tossing and turning in bed, no doubt contemplating the possibility that my acting debut would turn into a debacle—for her, for me, and for Performing Animal Troupe, whose reputation and future business prospects clearly were on the line.

As things turned out, however, Claire needn't have worried. In my very first movie scene I not only put her fears to rest, I showed my trainer/mom and the director the true meaning of the word "chill"—no mean feat, I might add, considering the gazillion-watt studio lights glaring down at me from their metallic perches. When given the signal by Claire, I licked Colin's face as if both of our lives depended on my reviving him. In fact, I licked it over and over again, since Martin McDonagh shot several takes of this (and every other scene). I did it because Colin's skin was smeared with pork-flavored baby food. I did it for the hugs I got after each successful take. Above all, I did it for my mom.

Chapter 8

The Nice Man Cometh

Don't tell anyone, but Woody Harrelson is really a very nice man.

COMING off that first week of shooting, I was feeling pretty good about myself. I had hit all of my marks, barked on command, looked adoringly at the actors who played sympathetic roles, while ignoring the ones my character was *not* supposed to like. It was right about then that an assistant director approached my mom, informing her that Woody Harrelson, who plays L.A. gangster "Charlie Costello" in the movie, wanted to meet with me later that afternoon. The actor needed to psych out why his character loves his little Lion Dog—coincidentally, also named "Bonny"—with such pugnacious fury he is willing to kill as many people as it might take to get him back from the men who snatched him, the event that sets the movie's plot in motion.

It amazed me how cool, calm and collected my mom remained after receiving this unexpected news. I didn't realize back then that suddenly being put on the spot like that happens all the time in the animal training business. Having worked one-on-one before with such big-name stars as George Clooney, Halle Berry, Britney Spears and Kevin Spacey, Claire took Woody Harrelson's request in stride. Because she was so calm, when we entered the house in L.A.'s Korea Town neighborhood together a few hours later that served as a kind of temporary on-deck circle for the actors on location, I was calm too.

Woody, who was seated on a couch, stood up and greeted Claire and me with a smile. The first thing each of us noticed was his eyes, these giant blue orbs that practically glowed with warmth and sincerity. So friendly, down-to-earth and relaxed was the actor, in fact, I found it hard to imagine him in his scary bad guy role.

"Hey there," he said, offering his hand to Claire. "I'm Woody—and you must be Claire—and this," he said, reaching out his arms for me, "must be little Bonny."

Whereupon he sat back down on the couch with me on his lap and began stroking me while chatting up Claire—more to put her at ease, I sensed, than to glean any practical information he might need for the movie's climactic scene— the first and only one in which he and I would appear together.

"So," he said to Claire like he'd just met her at a cocktail party or something and had all the time in the world to shoot the breeze with her, "how'd you happen to become an animal trainer?"

While my mom answered his question—briefly, because she understood his real purpose and need at that time was to get to know me—I laid back and enjoyed the ride, so to speak, inhaling his smell, getting used to the tone and timbre of his voice, the way he moved his body, the almost scary amount of energy I could feel emerging from it.

After my mom finished telling him about her path into the wrangler's life—which had begun after she interviewed a professional animal trainer in her native British Columbia at age 16—Woody did something I've witnessed only rarely in humans: He was comfortable enough in his own skin and with the stranger he'd just met to fall silent in her presence. He focused all of his attention on me. For the next quarter of an hour or so, with mom sitting nearby and looking on approvingly but not interfering in any way, Woody got into character and played with me as he imagined Charlie Costello might have done in the privacy of his home, out of sight and earshot of the fictitious bodyguards and hit men he employed, allowing him to tap into his sensitive "inner gangster." And so this thespian macho man proceeded to hug, tease, and tickle me. He even began babbling to me in baby talk, which made Claire blush, but my discreet trainer/mom was smart enough not to say anything to Woody —especially while he was channeling the very dark soul of Mr. Charlie Costello.

For my part, I got so excited by all the attention being showered on me by the wonderful new man in my life, I broke out of Woody's grasp and began hopping around on the couch, barking and wagging my tail like a love-crazed bunny rabbit, whereupon both the actor and the animal trainer broke out laughing, bringing a mirthful and harmonious end to our get-acquainted session.

After my mom leashed me up, Woody bid the two of us goodbye. Then he did something else

36

that I don't often see or hear on the movie sets I have visited or worked on with my mom: He sincerely thanked Claire for bringing me by and for so kindly giving him a half an hour of her time. As we drove back to the ranch together, I could hear Claire talking excitedly with Aunt Cathy (now that I'd grown closer to the lady who'd adopted me, I no longer used the more formal "Miss Cathy" appellation) about our meeting with Woody. She was pleased and I was pleased. I could barely wait till I got the chance to do my happy dance for the gentle, if rough-hewn, movie star again.

Chapter 9
Don't Shoot—I'm A Dog!

Sam Rockwell, whose character dognaps me, then shoots it out with Woody Harrelson in the California desert, holds me as he confers with writer/director Martin McDonagh at the October 2012 L.A. premiere of "Seven Psychopaths."

GUNS were blazing, bullets flying, bodies falling all around me. Yet in the midst of the chaos and carnage perpetrated by a multitude of villains in "Seven Psychopaths," this eleven-month-old, newly adopted Shih Tzu puppy remained totally calm. Even a car exploding and burning on the set failed to stir a whimper from me. Was I Superdog? No. I was well-trained, confident that my mom would protect me from harm, and gifted with an almost preternatural ability to ignore everything going on around me.

Did I mention that Claire had put cotton in my ears?

Having exactly zero rehearsal days in which to acclimate me to the loud noises that punctuate the action throughout the film, Claire, as animal trainers so often have to do on movie sets, had improvised. Fortunately, she also got some help from the special effects guys, who did a little shoot-em-up bang-bang exercise just for me. They fired their guns from a distance, then gradually worked their way closer to me. I'll admit I jumped a little on the first volley, looking at Claire as if to ask her: "Oh, my, what was *that*?"

I reacted similarly to the subsequent gunshots, but I never panicked. Which clearly pleased my mom. I think she was coming to picture me as a miniature canine version of Buster Keaton, the Great Stone Face comedian of the silent film era. No matter what happened to him in the story, he always responded stoically, with seemingly all of the world's sadness and futility reflected in those big, brown, doggie-like eyes. One night, Claire and I watched him in "The General," where he plays a train engineer during the Civil War. In my very favorite scene, he sits on the giant metal drive arm of his steam engine, which slowly begins lifting him up, then lowering him down, as the locomotive he is supposed to be driving chugs along the track with no one at the controls.

I never tried—or wanted—to equal this great actor's daredevil feats, but my unflappability on the movie set nearly got me burned—literally. Martin McDonagh was filming an outdoor scene in which "Billy" (Sam Rockwell) sets fire to the gas tank of his car, causing it to explode and burn. He does this to force "Hans" (Christopher Walken) and "Marty" (Colin Farrell) to stay with him and help him ambush "Charlie Costello" (Woody Harrelson) when he comes to rescue me. I was not actually in this scene, but in the previous one Marty had tied me to a post about 100 yards from the soon-to-be flaming sedan. It was a particularly cold and windy day on location in the California desert. Somehow, I managed to slip out of the tether and began heading for the burning car, hoping to warm my chilled little body by getting closer to the flames. I'd never seen a fire before and didn't know it could harm you. But before I got very far, Colin Farrell spotted me and came running up.

"You rascal!" he said, snatching me up off the sand. Then he brought me to Claire, who had also been hot on my trail. She took me in her arms, looking really shook up.

Before the day's filming was done, I escaped from my tether once again and reprised my heat-seeking act. This time, Claire herself rescued me, but did not appear to be quite as amused as Colin had been. I probably shouldn't admit this, but I enjoyed stirring her up. Sometimes, a dog has to do something crazy like that to get her human's attention. The test need not be a life-and-death matter, but it's important to remind our two-legged parents from time to time of just how lucky they are to have us in their lives.

Chapter 10
We Got Zen

In the movie, Christopher Walken, a.k.a. "Hans," dognaps me and holds me for ransom. In real life, however, he was kind to me and bragged to reporters about my acting chops.

TO paraphrase one of Hollywood's most beloved figures, the late, great Will Rogers, I never met a man—or a woman—during the shooting of "Seven Psychopaths," I did not like. If you'd been on the set with me, you'd understand. Everyone from the director on down to the lowest-ranking member of the production crew seemed to take an interest in me. Whether that meant a wink and a smile, a quick head tickle, a treat or some serious cuddling, I found myself at the center of a loving universe that was as real to me as the make-believe world being painstakingly created around me by these very same folks. Although I appreciated each and every one of them in his or her own right, like any other flawed yet thoughtful creature I liked and responded to some people more readily than others.

A few days into the filming, the movie's first assistant director, named Peter, kind of discovered me. Every day from them on, the second most powerful and probably busiest human on the set would take the time to say hello. Naturally, I didn't want to be too transparent about how much I enjoyed the cuddles and attention he gave me, but, just between you and me, it was very nice. After a while, he became so attached to me that other crew members looking for him to solve their latest problem would joke to one another: "If you want to find Peter, just look for Bonny. He won't be far away."

Part way through the filming, Peter asked Claire if I had a home to go to after the filming was done. If not, he wanted to adopt me. His request, by the way, was not unusual. Peter knew that, like so many movie dogs, I was rehomed, and that Aunt Cathy had acquired me only recently for my role in "Seven Psychopaths." For all he knew, this would be my first, last, and only strut before the cameras.

During the filming, everyone was very nice to me, including writer-director Martin McDonagh, who let me sit on his special chair.

Aunt Cathy considered the idea. Peter had a wife and kids and he clearly loved me, so she knew I would be in a good home. But, I'm happy and sad to say, she ultimately turned down his request. Happy because I ended up with Claire, sad because I knew Peter and his family were disappointed that they could not adopt me.

Another crew member, hair stylist Pauletta, became so enamored of this four-legged film actress that she gave me a present—something Claire says never had happened before during any of her movie or TV shoots. It was a round metal collar tag with a flower on it and an inscription reading: "Am I cute or what?" Knowing it came straight from this sweet lady's heart, I gratefully accepted it with a wiggle and a kiss. In fact, I've grown so attached to this memento, if my mom ever tried to remove it from my collar, I might have to break my perfect record of nonaggression against my fellow living beings and sink my teeth into her. (Just kidding, Mom, I would never bite the hand that feeds me!)

There was somebody else on that movie set— one of the lead actors, it so happens—who seemed to vibrate on the exact same wavelength as me. From the moment we played our first scene together to the final day of shooting with Christopher Walken, who plays the quirky leader of an L.A. dognapping ring named "Hans," I could sense I was dealing with a fellow traveler. There is something cat-like about Chris, which also can be said about the Shih Tzu. Though private and mysterious, almost Sphinx-like, we can be friendly when it suits us and clearly are comfortable in our own skin. We can accept— even honor—other people and animals without actually acknowledging that we need them. And, as my mom will attest—at least with regard to me —we are a total pain in the butt to train.

Our mutual attraction became obvious to everyone when we were shooting a scene in which "Hans," "Billy" (Sam Rockwell), and "Marty" (Colin Farrell) had stopped at a Los Angeles pub on their way to the desert, where the final showdown with "Charlie Costello" and his gang would take place. Sam put me onto the table, whereupon I walked over to where Chris was sitting and mimicked his expression like little Jackie Coogan in Charlie Chaplin's classic movie, "The Kid." The move wasn't in the script, but Marty McDonagh seemed to like my spontaneous acting riff, because he kept it in the final cut.

Between takes, Chris came up to where Claire and I were seated on a bench next to a wall and sat down next to us. "This is the greatest dog I ever worked with," he told her, as he petted me. The eccentric, but brilliant, veteran thespian said that he really liked working with me because I was "very natural," allowing him and the other actors just to be themselves, and to relate to me as just a friendly little dog, rather than a more formally trained "canine actor." He suggested this more natural approach would come across as far more believable on screen.

Chris then admitted to Claire that, though he likes dogs, he is more of a "cat person." He said he had noticed, while working with me, that I too am quiet and "cat-like" and that I have a sort of Zen-like, introspective quality about me. He had noticed that, whenever I wasn't actually on camera, I would go off into my own little world, obviously thinking about stuff. This seemed to confirm what he'd heard about the Shih Tzu's high level of intelligence. All good, Chris, *all good*!

I appeared with Chris, Sam and Colin in another bar scene—this one shot in Venice, California—just before Christmas 2011. Regrettably, it happened to be Chris's last day on the set. After the final take, he came up to Claire and me and gave both of us a hug. I would not see my cat-like friend again until the international premier of "Seven Psychopaths" in Toronto, Ontario, almost a year later, where he would prove his love for me by protecting me from an overzealous fan.

Chapter 11
It's A Wrap!

Girls just wanna have fun!

TURNS out that when humans finish a big piece of communal work—shooting a feature film, for example—they like to come together and eat, drink, talk, dance, kiss, hug, shout, reminisce, and otherwise celebrate the great thing they have achieved together. In Hollywood, they call this the "wrap party."

The one for "Seven Psychopaths" was held at a private club in L.A., whose manager, despite pleas for an exception to be made by my mom and several crew members, refused to allow me to set paw inside the food-serving indoor portion of the establishment. "I have nothing against dogs," he explained, in a futile attempt to rationalize his obvious species discrimination. Only hominids, he asserted, are allowed by local health regulations to mingle in the enclosed part of this elite location. Don't the statute's authors know that a dog's mouth is like a gazillion times cleaner than a person's? I mean, who would you rather be bitten by—me or, say, Mike Tyson, who once chomped off a piece of his astonished opponent's ear during a world championship boxing match? (It's an easy choice, n'est-ce pas?)

Naturally, my mom was burned up by this unexpected development; but, being a polite, cooperative, and adaptive human, she not only accepted the situation with her usual good grace (in other words, she did not make a scene), she pretty much had the last laugh on the misguided manager and the local health officials who'd dreamt up those restrictions by holding court with me on the outdoor patio adjoining the club's indoor lounge.

As the night progressed, just about every crew member came by at some point to say hello/goodbye to Claire and me. I got so much attention that I rarely touched the ground: If

Claire wasn't holding me in her arms, somebody else was. Those who greeted us included the film's first assistant director, Peter, and its hairstylist, Pauletta, who had closely bonded with me during the production. But some people I didn't know nearly as well also made a point of saying hi and/or reminiscing about the experience they had shared with Claire and me. I think they found it hard to resist checking out both me and my dolled-up mom. That night, I was decked out in the dress once worn by a Pomeranian named "Quigley" in the movie, "Welcome Home, Roscoe Jenkins!" ("Quigley" is a boy but, like me, he 'switched genders' for his movie role.) Aunt Cathy had worked on that production and the dress, along with other outfits worn by the four-legged actor, had been given to her as a gift at the end of it. She had made the shiny red gown, which is sprinkled with hearts, available to Claire and me for this special occasion.

At one point during the evening, director Marty McDonagh called everyone together to show us some rough-cut scenes from the movie. There on a wide-screen television screen was this little dog that was the spitting image of me. In fact, she looked just like the creature I once had spied in mom's bedroom closet mirror, the one who purposely had done everything I was doing—only with the opposite paw—obviously intent on mocking and provoking me. Meanwhile, I could see that the Shih Tzu in the movie clearly had done a splendid job of following her cues, barking, holding up her paw, licking or walking away from an actor at precisely the moment called for in the script. I remember doing similar things on a movie set during the wonderful adventure I had shared with my mom at the end of my first year of life. But I also knew instinctively that it is impossible to be in two places at once. If I truly was sitting here in this exclusive club looking at a TV screen with the assembled crew members, how could I also be inside that TV screen, playing off those human actors? It was all too much for my little doggie brain to comprehend. I decided to let those with larger craniums figure out such complex conundrums. I will stick with my simpler but no less important role of charming and befriending everyone I meet. This is both the destiny and the duty of the Shih Tzu, sealed by a sacred ancestral vow to which I shall always remain true.

Chapter 12
The New Normal

Lola is the only four-legged soul I totally trust—
although sometimes she really gets on my nerves.

ONCE the filming was done, I began spending
a lot more time with Aunt Cathy and Uncle Gregg
in California's dry, windy, dusty high-desert

country north of L.A, as my mom would bring me
with her when she went there to work. I love their
little spread, which is located in a town called
Palmdale. When you first arrive at "the Ranch,"
which is headquarters for Performing Animal
Troupe, you're greeted by a cheerful, desert-style
landscape featuring a little rock river, spraying
fountains, antique wagon wheels planted in the
sand, and a quaintly painted brick wall.
Sometimes, Claire would leave me there for a few
days when she was on an out of-town
assignment. On those occasions, I would spend
most of my time with Aunt Cathy and Uncle
Gregg's twenty-something son, Justin, whose
room is at the back of the house. He's an easy-
going guy, doesn't mind if I just lie around doing
my own thing, and he has a really cool fish tank
with lots of exotic creatures swimming around in
it. When I wanted a change of scenery, I would
hang out in the rustically decorated great room,
sprawled on the red tile floor Aunt Cathy and
Uncle Gregg imported from Mexico. If there
happened to be logs blazing in the big brick
fireplace, it seemed like the closest this little Shih
Tzu would ever get to heaven.

Although the Ranch covers only a few acres, it
is home to all manner of birds and beasts, any
one of whom can be—and many of whom already
have been—called upon to go before the camera.
Thus, if I wanted to, in addition to the company's
dozens of working dogs, I could intimately

acquaint myself with any of the Pittmans' well-loved and well trained horses, donkeys, llamas, goats, sheep, rabbits, pigeons and parrots, to name just some of the species in their ever-changing menagerie. Like me, nearly all were rescued by Aunt Cathy and Uncle Gregg, who believe that rehomed animals naturally make better actors. In their eyes, not only are we grateful for being given a fresh lease on life, we often have feisty personalities—one reason our previous owners might not have been able to handle us—and are eager to please the humans who adopted us. We want to show them that the talents they perceived in us are real.

Still, regardless of their acting abilities, I had no desire to hang out with most of my fellow nonhumans at the Ranch, even the dogs, who had quite the backyard setup, which included a custom-built doghouse, an array of toys, even kiddie pools for cooling off and slaking their thirst in the high-desert heat. Whereas the dogs simply didn't interest me, the other species husbanded by Aunt Cathy and Uncle Gregg—especially those so big you could fit maybe a thousand Shih Tzu inside one of them—flat out unnerved me. Hoping to avoid contact with both the canines and the larger or more exotic animals, and having developed a pretty high comfort level with guys during the shooting of "Seven Psychopaths," whenever I was at the Ranch I parked my paws with Justin.

The funny thing is, he generally paid very little attention to me. Which was fine with me. Even when I'm with people, I'm frequently in my own little world, thinking my Shih Tzu thoughts, dreaming my Lion Dog dreams. Indeed, hanging out with friendly, caring humans such as Justin and his pals, who acknowledge my presence without hassling me with unwanted attention, is the ideal setup for me.

And so my post-cinematic life settled into a pleasant, reassuring rhythm. When I wasn't at Aunt Cathy's or on assignment with my mom (who sometimes took me on local shoots with other animals she handles), I got to hang out at Claire's smaller ranch house in a town not far from Palmdale. More and more lately, that meant spending time with Lola. The scruffy Chihuahua/terrier mix is the only one of Claire's seven dogs who is smaller than me, and the only one I have ever tried to interact with. (Claire also has cats, but I totally ignore them.) It's not just that Lola is pound for pound the least threatening of the pack, she's also a friendly, tolerant, endearing soul who "gets" me. Happily, when I first pounced on her with my two front paws, she understood that I was trying to play. Soon, we were wrestling and play-fighting together like a pair of puppies (which I, of course, still was). Our tentative *paws de deux* eventually transformed into a bond of trust second only to that forged between my mom and me. Today, my BFLF and I are practically inseparable; occasionally, we even sleep snuggled up next to one another in one of the many doggie beds Claire has placed around the house to comfort us whenever the Sandman calls.

But as much as I love Lola, as happens so often in affairs of the heart, there is a downside to our closeness. I sometimes get jealous of her. When my mom goes overboard in handing out treats or attention to her, I bark my dissatisfaction. "Hey!" I remind her, "As cute and sweet as Miss Lola is, can't you see I'm even *more* loveable and adorable?"

I want to be No. 1 on Claire's Doggie Hit Parade, not No. 2 or No. 3. I don't know if it's my regal Shih Tzu nature that makes me feel that way, or the residual insecurity that comes from being rehomed. I just know that, if I have to yodel every now and then in order to remind my mom that I am the natural center of her universe, then that's what I will do.

Chapter 13
Birth Of A Salesgirl

At the L.A. premiere of "Seven Psychopaths,"
all the stars, including yours truly, got to pose
in front of this poster.

THE paparazzi were held back only by a flimsy red velvet rope as I sat, a few feet away, on the red carpet laid along the brick alleyway outside the theater in Toronto, Ontario, where "Seven Psychopaths" was having its North American premiere. It was September 7, 2012, nearly a year after my acting debut. I was on my first publicity tour, which was proving almost as stressful and weird as the wildest days of filming, when people were shooting each other and blowing up cars in a humongous fight over me.

Now, they were blinding me with their camera lights.

"Bonny, look at me!" a photographer shouted.

"Smile for the camera!" yelled another.

"Over here, Bonny!"

Despite their implorations, however, I ignored the lens men and ladies, focusing only on Claire, who was kneeling nearby, giving me the hand signal for "stay where you are, kid, and continue to chill." I kept my cool even as a series of limos began to pull up nearby, disgorging their celebrity passengers. One gave up Christopher Walken. After taking his required stroll past the camera wielders and greeting a gaggle of enraptured fans, my cat-like bud addressed the entertainment scribes gathered behind another velvet rope.

As Chris regaled them, Sam Rockwell, whose German Shepherd, Sadie, had visited him on the set during the filming (I gave her a wide berth), came up to Claire and asked if he could "borrow" me for a moment.

Sam Rockwell and girlfriend Leslie Bibb
walk their German Shepard Sadie, who
one day appeared on the movie set.

Trailed by my mom (she never lets me out of her sight when we're working), Sam carried me over to his co-star and placed me in Chris's arms.

The actor who had once told Claire I was the greatest dog he'd ever worked with, greeted me

59

warmly. For several minutes, Chris continued his playful give-and-take with the journalists. But then he suddenly tensed up, making my own heart race sympathetically. Glaring at the reporter who had just shouted a question at him, he suddenly handed me to Claire.

Unbeknownst to either of us at the time, Chris had nearly come to blows with this fellow —over yours truly! Later, he would explain to a USA Today reporter: "It was hot with these flashbulbs going off. There was this huge guy standing next to me yelling, 'Let me pick her up.' And I'm protecting the dog, thinking, 'If you touch that dog, I will crack you right in the face'."

Fortunately, no blows were exchanged, but I have to admit it was nice to learn later that Chris —a pseudo-tough guy who's really a softie at heart—had been ready to defend this canine actress from potential danger. Claire has said more than once that she would pull a 'Charlie Costello' on anyone who tried to take me away from her or otherwise threatened me, but, frankly, with all due respect to my mom, if it came down to fisticuffs, I'm afraid I'd have to bet my kibbles on the bad guy.

While in Toronto, I also did half a dozen media interviews, barking my response to such inquiries as "What was it like to work with Woody Harrelson?" and "You gotta itch? I do too." My favorite appearance was with Jimmy O. on JoBlo.com. A video of this interview is at: www.youtube.com/watch?v=Xbt8vhWdQt8.

In a September 2012 interview, I barked to Jimmy O. about working with Woody Harrelson, second from right, posing here with writer/director Martin McDonagh, wearing a tie, and several of my human co-stars in Toronto.

Strange as it may seem to those unfamiliar with the movie biz, there was a second premiere of "Seven Psychopaths" about three weeks later. This one, marking the film's U.S. release, was staged at the funky and historic Mann Bruin Theatre in Westwood, California. To make us easily available to the press, the producers put the cast members up at the Beverly Hills Hilton.

*Contrary to popular belief, as anyone can see from this picture, mimicry is **not** always the highest form of flattery.*

When Claire and I arrived at our room, we found two brand new doggie bowls, one containing gourmet dog food (it was yummy!), the other a bottle of Fiji water. The producers also had left us a publicity kit, a cardboard dog carrier decorated with the movie logo. Inside was a funny little hat with earflaps identical to the one Sam Rockwell wore in the movie, and a stuffed animal that was supposed to look like me, but didn't. Not even close. To show my displeasure, I got ahold of the poodle-looking thing with my teeth and shook the stuffing out of it.

Shortly before the screening, my co-stars and I strolled along a black carpet flanked by giant blow-ups of the movie posters the producers had created to help publicize the film, including one showing me being held by Sam and reading: "He does not take any Shih Tzu."

Sharon Osbourne comforts me, while scolding her husband, rocker Ozzie Osbourne, after he pretended to strangle me to amuse the photographers.

In addition to the cast, a number of Tinsel Town celebrities attended the premiere. They included rocker Ozzie Osbourne and his wife, Sharon, a well-known dog lover who asked Claire if she could hold me. When mom complied, Ozzie hammed it up for the photographers by pretending to strangle me. I did not react.

By that point, even my mom had to admit that the extraordinary calmness I displayed—at the premieres, and earlier, during the filming—transcended anything she might have taught me. She attributes this to my ability to "tune out everything" around me. Truth be told, the roots of this behavior go far deeper than the personality of this particular Shih Tzu. In fact, they go back more than two thousand years to a time when my ancestor, the original Lion Dog, served as a guardian and companion to the Buddha during the great Indian mystic's travels along the Ganges River plain. Apparently, being that close to the calmest, most centered being on the planet affected my ancestor so profoundly that even his humblest and most distant descendants, such as yours truly, still display those same, Buddha-like traits today.

Me, on the black carpet in L.A.

Chapter 14

Beyond The Red Carpet

Me, sharing the love with military veterans near the
World War Two Memorial in Washington, D.C.

MORE than two years have passed since I was plucked from obscurity in an East L.A. trailer park through the miracle of Craigslist and transformed virtually overnight into a canine movie star. (Gone are the days when a girl like me was more likely to be discovered by a talent scout lingering near the soda fountain at Schwab's Drug Store.) Although I would relish the chance to work on another movie–an experience that opened so many new doors to me—my life outside the hustle and flow of Tinsel Town has been anything but tame. Since the cameras stopped rolling on my first feature film, I have appeared in print and TV ads for such well-known national brands as Petco, Skechers shoes, and, oddly enough, *Readers Digest*. I also was featured in a comedy skit on Jimmy Kimmel Live, and I got to strut my funky stuff down the runway at *Le Chien Couture*, the doggie fashion show held in March 2013 in Palm Desert, California.

Me, getting ready to play my part in a nationally televised comedy skit.

Of course, many readers know these things about me and more, since my mom faithfully posts news of my accomplishments on the Facebook page she has created for me at www.facebook.com/BonnyShihTzu, along with my latest photos (even nap time is fair game for my picture-loving mom!) I'm grateful to note that, as of April 2014, over four thousand very special people—possibly including *you*, dear reader—have "liked" me on Facebook.

But even some of my Facebook fans may not remember that, in April 2013, I traveled to the nation's capital with Barbara Gordon to help promote the pet therapy dog program she founded, called R.O.M.P., which stands for Reconnecting with Our Military Personnel. We appeared on a television program, "The Pet Show With Dr. Katy," and we visited the World War Two Memorial on the National Mall. There I had the privilege of meeting some distinguished members of America's "Greatest Generation." Whenever one of these aging heroes picked me up, I'll admit my heart beat a little faster.

Also in 2013, which turned out to be my busiest year ever, two authors—Jonathan Agronsky, who is helping me with this book, and Kyra Sundance—devoted entire chapters to me in their books, *Shih Tzu Nation: America Falls for the Lion Dog* and *101 Dog Tricks: Kids Edition*, respectively. (You can find more information about *Shih Tzu Nation* at www.shihtzunation.com

and more about *101 Dog Tricks: Kids Edition* at www.qbookshop.com/products/21304/978.)

And I am the featured pinup girl for every single month in the 2014 calendar my mom produced to help raise money for Aunt Cathy's animal rescue organization, Old Friends Shelter and Education Center, Inc. (You can purchase the calendar at www.bonnytheshihtzu.com.)

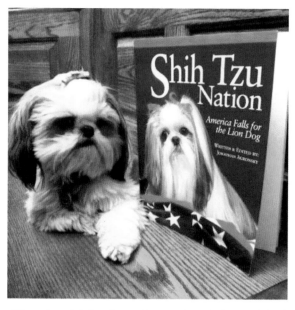

Chapter 10 in Jonathan's book is entitled "Seven Psychopaths and a Shih Tzu." I'll bet you can guess who it's about!

Perhaps my greatest honor came from the American Humane Association, which presented me with its 2013 Pawscar Award for Best Animal in a Leading Role. Describing me as the "epicenter" of "Seven Psychopaths," the animal welfare group credited me with "moving the plot forward while attracting the attention of every character in this rollicking farce." Not bad, wouldn't you agree, for a newly trained walk-on?

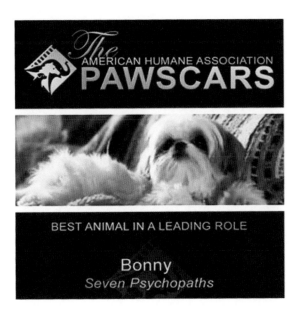

As great as it feels to receive such kudos, however, I have discovered something completely outside the entertainment and merchandising worlds that is even more gratifying: serving the men and women who once served our country under arms. Early in 2013, I was tested and certified as a therapy dog through the volunteer group Actors and Others for Animals. Since then, I have paid several visits to a Department of Veterans Affairs Ambulatory Care Center in L.A., along with my mom and R.O.M.P. founder Barbara Gordon. Usually, we meet the patients in the facility's day room, where they gather to watch television, play cards or board games, chat with one another, or just sit there and chill.

Me and mom at the Department of Veterans Affairs Ambulatory Care Center in Los Angeles, where I serve as a volunteer therapy dog.

Since Barbara must take the lead in such encounters—until my mom becomes certified as a therapy dog handler—she will approach an

70

individual patient and ask him or her (mostly "hims") if he would like to interact with me. Almost everyone says yes. When Barbara plops me onto a patient's lap, I don't like jump up and start wagging my tail or doing a happy little puppy dance or anything. I just do my Zen Shih Tzu thing: I lie there calmly, allowing him to pet me. If he happens to speak, I look directly into his eyes as if what he is saying is the most fascinating and important thing I have heard in all of my days. Which seems to make these aging heroes happy. (I know it makes me happy.)

And so I progress, one lap at a time, around the day room, touching the hearts and minds of strangers. It seems this is my fate, whether I act it out on a movie set or up close and personal. I did not seek out this destiny. It chose me. But I have had the wisdom and humility to embrace it. And in that simple act of surrender lies the secret of my, and perhaps all dogs', happiness and contentment. That and the special bonds we forge with those at the center of our universe. With Claire and Lola by my side, there is no challenge I will not take on, no human or reasonably sized four-legged creature I will not befriend (unless it's a cat).

Bring on the next adventure!

PHOTO CREDITS

ABOUT THE AUTHORS

FROM her humble beginnings in an East L.A. trailer park to her current status as one of America's premier acting dogs, **Bonny the Shih Tzu** has never lost sight of either her Shih Tzu roots or her primary mission in life, which is to charm, comfort, and amuse everyone she encounters. Today, the three-year-old Lion Dog, owned by Performing Animal Troupe, lives with her mom, animal trainer Claire Doré, six other dogs and a bunch of obnoxious cats in California's Antelope Valley north of L.A.

SMALL dogs with ponytails used to freak out Bonny's co-author, **Jonathan Agronsky**, shown here with his second Shih Tzu, Poppy, until his then-girlfriend (now life partner) Bonnie Fitzpatrick brought home an adorable gold-and-white fluff ball she would call Sasha in February 1987. That Valentine Day's surprise eventually changed the way the Washington, D.C. native saw not just little dogs but all of God's creatures, great and small, including himself. Jonathan currently lives with Bonnie and their spirited red-and-white girl in East-central North Carolina.

Made in the USA
Lexington, KY
31 August 2014